THE

FEDERAL RESERVE ACT

OF 1913

HISTORY AND DIGEST

by

V. GILMORE IDEN

PUBLISHED BY

THE NATIONAL BANK NEWS

PHILADELPHIA

History

ON MONDAY, October 21, 1907, the National Bank of Commerce of New York City announced its refusal to clear for the Knickerbocker Trust Company of the same city. The trust company had deposits amounting to $62,000,000. The next day, following a run of three hours, the Knickerbocker Trust Company paid out $8,000,000 and then suspended.

One immediate result was that banks, acting independently, held on tight to the cash they had in their vaults, and money went to a premium. According to the experts who investigated the situation, this panic was purely a bankers' panic and due entirely to our system of banking, which bases the protection of the financial solidity of the country upon the individual reserves of banks. In the case of a stress, such as in 1907, the banks fail to act as a whole, their first consideration being the protection of their own reserves.

The conditions surrounding previous panics were entirely different. In 1873 the currency was inconvertible and depreciated, and the banks could not increase their available cash reserve by the acquisition of gold. About twenty years later silver purchases weakened the monetary structure and caused distrust of American securities at home and abroad. The panic of 1907 was not preceded by any legislative disturbances or monetary unsoundness.

This panic was preceded by a season of greatest prosperity. It was followed by a widespread demand for currency reform. What economic students had been urging for a long time at last, as a result of this panic, culminated in the appointment of a National Monetary Commission by Congress and ultimately in the Federal Reserve Act of 1913. A study of monetary conditions was authorized by a Republican administration, and remedial legislation was enacted by a Democratic administration.

The immediate result of this panic was the enactment of a temporary measure known as the Aldrich-Vreeland emergency currency act, which was to expire by limitation on June 30, 1914. This act permitted the incorporation of national banks into associations similar to clearing houses and the issuance of "emergency" currency in times of stress upon certain securities approved by the authority of these associations and the government, which securities could be other than government bonds.

It was some time before the banks would organize under the authority of this act, the claim being made that the law would not work. Finally the Secretary of the Treasury during the Taft administration persuaded the banks in a number of the cities to organize. This, it was believed, was merely for the purpose of a pretense, as no one ever contemplated that the terms of the temporary act would be put into practice, and experience since has proven the truth of this prediction.

The National Monetary Commission was composed of Nelson W. Aldrich, of Rhode Island, chairman; Edward B. Vreeland, of New York, vice chairman; Julius C. Burrows, of Michigan; Eugene Hale, of Maine; H. M. Teller, of Colorado; H. D. Money, of Mississippi; Theodore E. Burton, of Ohio; Jas. P. Taliaferro, of Florida; Boise Penrose, of Pennsylvania; John W. Weeks, of Massachusetts; Robert W. Bonynge, of Colorado; L. P. Padgett, of Tennessee; Geo. F. Burgess, of Texas; A. P. Pujo, of Louisiana; Geo. W. Prince, of Illinois, and Jas. McLachlan, of California. A. Piatt Andrew, of Massachusetts, later Assistant Secretary of the Treasury during the Taft administration, was employed as an assistant to the commission and did most of the formulative work of that body.

The commission conducted investigations and held hearings in this country and abroad. The greater part of the energies of the commission, however, were expended in collecting an adequate working library. Volumes on the various banking systems of the world were prepared by the leading economic students of the countries in question, and all were published by the commission. Because of the large monetary outlay made in this direction the Democrats criticized the commission very severely.

The National Monetary Commission, upon investigation, discovered the principal defects in our banking system to be in that:

"1: We have no provision for the concentration of the cash reserves of the banks and for their mobilization and use wherever needed in times of trouble. Experience has shown that the scattered cash reserves of our banks are inadequate for purposes of assistance or defense at such times.

"2. Antiquated Federal and State laws restrict the use of bank reserves and prohibit the lending power of banks at times when, in the presence of unusual demands, reserves should be freely used and credit liberally extended to all deserving customers.

"3. Our banks also lack adequate means available for use at any time to replenish their reserves or increase their loaning powers when necessary to meet normal or unusual demands."

There were seventeen of these "principal" defects in all, but this number will suffice to indicate the remedy which would naturally be proposed. In company with Dr. Andrew, Senator Aldrich finally drafted a plan to remedy the conditions. It was strictly Senator Aldrich's plan, but the Monetary Commission gave it the stamp of approval. As later appearing in the report of the commission, the plan was as follows:

"It is proposed to incorporate the National Reserve Association of the United States with an authorized capital equal to 20 per cent of the capital of all subscribing banks, of which one-half shall be paid in and the remainder shall become a liability, subject to call * * * *. It is also provided that before the reserve association can commence business, $100,000,000 of capital must be paid in cash. All State banks and trust companies conforming to the provisions of the bill with reference to capitalization and reserves and all National banks are entitled to subscribe for stock and to become members of the association. Shares in the association are not transferable and can not be owned otherwise than by a subscribing bank or in any other than the proportion named.

"It is proposed to group into local associations all subscribing banks located in contiguous territory. The local associations are to be organized into district associations, in each of which shall be located a branch of the National Reserve Association; and the district associations, which shall be so arranged as to include all the territory of the United States, are combined to form the National Reserve Association of the United States.

"One of the principal functions of the local associations is to guarantee, upon application, the commercial paper of individual banks which may be offered to the branches for rediscount * * * *.

The local association may, and in most cases would, require from the bank making the application satisfactory security for the guarantee. Local associations are authorized in serious emergencies to guarantee the direct obligations of subscribing banks with adequate security * * * *. A local association may decline to give the guarantees provided for under either of these sections. Local associations may also, by vote of three-fourths of their board of directors and the approval of the National Reserve Association, assume and exercise the powers and functions of clearing houses. They are required also to perform such services in facilitating domestic exchanges as, in the opinion of the National Reserve Association, the public interests may require."

Speaking elsewhere in the report, the proposed association was described as follows:

"It is not a bank, but a co-operative union of all the banks of the country, with very limited and clearly defined functions. First, it holds a portion of the cash reserves of the banks of the United States, with the provision for their use only for specific purposes; second, it is granted the power to issue circulating notes under strict governmental regulations; third, through the maintenance of its own reserves and the character and extent of its resources, it is required to sustain the credit of the banks and of the country under all circumstances. All of its operations are confined to, or incidental to these purposes, the only exception being the transaction of its business as the fiscal agent of the government of the United States."

When the Democrats gained control of the House of Representatives in the political elections of 1910, the offices being filled in 1911, they forced the National Monetary Commission to make its report and wind up its work. In making this report, Senator Aldrich outlined a plan for establishing a National Reserve Association, with regional institutions as indicated above. Immediately the Democrats attacked this as being typically republican and a plan that would tend further to concentrate the control of money in Wall Street. Many substitute Democratic plans for monetary reform were offered by the leaders of the party.

Beyond occasional discussion of the subject, the banking question was not again brought to the front until the Democratic platform of 1912 was adopted in Baltimore. Concerning banking legislation, this platform said:

"We oppose the so-called Aldrich bill, of the establishment of a Central Bank, and we believe the people of the country will be largely freed from panics and consequent unemployment and business depression by such a systematic revision of our banking laws as will render temporary relief in localities where such relief is needed, with protection from control or domination by what is known as the Money Trust.

"Banks exist for the accommodation of the public and not for the control of business. All legislation on the subject of banking and currency should have for its purpose the securing of these accommodations on terms of absolute security to the public and of complete protection from the misuse of the power that wealth gives to those who possess it.

"We condemn the present methods of depositing Government funds in a few favored banks, largely situated in or controlled by Wall Street, in return for political favors, and we pledge our party to provide by law for their deposit by competitive bidding in the banking institutions of the country, National or State, without discrimination as to locality, upon approved securities, and subject to call by the government."

While Chairman Pujo, of the House Banking and Currency Committee, was, with the aid of Attorney Samuel Untermyer, of New York, attempting to unearth sensational data relative to the existence of a Money Trust, Carter Glass, of Virginia, with his sub-committee from the same committee, was giving serious consideration to real banking legislation. Because of the bizarre nature of the Money Trust probe, but little was said of the Glass Committee, and thereby the country generally heard very little about the plans for constructive legislation.

Mr. Glass called a notable array of witnesses, including bankers from the most important financial centers and monetary experts. The short session of Congress came to an end on March 4, 1913, and the extra session was called April 7 of the same year by President Wilson to consider tariff revision.

Members of Congress are not students of finance, but rather students of politics. That is why it is so difficult for a scholar of finance to fathom out the reasons for the interesting fight made over the currency bill in the first and second sessions of the 63rd Congress. For the same reason those students of politics who did all the fighting were unable to fully understand the financial problem which they were supposed to be remedying by legislation.

In the spring of 1913 the newspapers began to publish reports that Carter Glass, the ranking Democrat on the House Banking and Currency Committee, had drafted a currency bill to be proposed to the President and Congress. As a matter of fact, there was some doubt for a time whether Mr. Glass would receive the chairmanship of that committee. Finally precedent prevailed and Mr. Glass was named chairman. H. Parker Willis, an economic student, it was later discovered, had drafted a currency bill for Mr. Glass. Dr. Willis was then in the employ of Mr. Glass as a monetary expert. The bill which the newspapers attributed to Mr. Glass was really the bill drafted by Dr. Willis. Following the elections of 1912, Mr. Glass and Dr. Willis had frequently gone to Trenton, N. J., for conferences with President-elect Wilson on this matter. It was presumed that they were, consequently, working in the interest of the new Democratic executive.

Only one thing stood in the way. That was the tariff legislation, which was a party promise.

So until this was assured, the President withheld his consent to make a fight for currency legislation. Consequently it was not until August 29 that the currency bill was first introduced. This bill bore the name of the Glass-Owen bill, because in its final shape it was the result of conferences between Mr. Glass, the President, Secretary of the Treasury McAdoo, Secretary of State Bryan and Senator Owen, chairman of the newly organized Banking and Currency Committee of the Senate.

Inasmuch as the bill was the joint product of the leaders of both houses and the recognized responsible persons in the Democratic party, it was to be expected that it would be easy to get it through Congress. Such was not the case, however. Representative Henry, of Texas, organized an insurgent move against the bill. Mr. Henry, it was reported, had a quarrel with the White House and hoped in this manner to square matters. He obtained the support of Representative Ragsdale, of South Carolina, and Representative Wingo, of Arkansas, both members of the Banking and Currency Committee and both new members in Congress. The Texas Congressman based his fight upon the demand for so-called "agricultural" currency. He said that, inasmuch as the proposed bill provided for asset currency, it should permit a farmer to store his agricultural products in warehouses and receive loans on the warehouse receipts.

Only the Democratic members of the House committee met to consider the bill introduced by Mr. Glass, but the first meeting resulted in almost a riot. It was impossible to accomplish anything. Several meetings were wasted in a fruitless discussion of procedure. Finally, as a result of pressure from the White House the Democrats agreed upon a report on the bill, but the insurgents forced a caucus. As a result of the caucus, which lasted over a week, all the Democrats came together, and Mr. Henry retired from the field of opposition. The Republican members of the committee were called in and a formal vote on the bill was taken. This resulted in a report to the House on September 9, where the measure was perfunctorily debated and finally adopted on September 18 by a vote of 286 to 85.

The action of the House of Representatives was so speedy that the country had hardly had time to fully understand the measure that the new Democratic administration was forcing upon it. The Senate had especially created a new committee, the Committee on Banking and Currency, to consider this measure, and placed at the head of it Senator Robert L. Owen, of Oklahoma. Senator Owen had made repeated attempts to call his committee together ever since the bill was introduced in the House, but without success. The members of the Senate committee were opposed to precipitated action.

In August a hurried call of the American Bankers' Association was convened in Chicago and a committee of bankers elected to wait upon Congress. This committee was given definite instructions as to what features of the bill to oppose. The bankers were permitted to appear before the Senate committee the first of September.

This again brought forth some criticism from the White House and the chairman of the House banking committee, Mr. Glass. It was insisted that the sole objection of the bankers to the House bill was that it contemplated the shifting of bank reserves, and to this only the large banks in the reserve cities were opposed. The President was unwilling that the Senate committee should delay action long enough to listen to the arguments of the bankers, but he failed to obtain his wish as completely as he did in the House.

The opening of hearings before the Senate committee brought forth many witnesses who clamored to be heard. The hearings stretched through September and well up into October. The printed records of these hearings covered many times the number of pages as did the hearings before the

House committee. The hearings were more complete than the hearings on the House side because the witnesses had a definite proposition before them to discuss. Before these were completed a second convention of bankers, more especially for the country banks, was held in Boston, at which another delegation was sent to oppose certain features of the bill before the Senate committee.

The country bankers had many and varied complaints to make. They opposed anything like a free clearing house for checks, they opposed the large subscription to stock of the reserve banks by country banks and they opposed the establishment of savings departments and the segregation of capital. But it was not until the concluding days of the hearing that the most dramatic moment was witnessed.

Frank A. Vanderlip, of the National City Bank, New York City, reappeared as a witness before the committee, and offered a comprehensive plan for the establishment of a central reserve bank, owned by the public and banks jointly and controlled by the government. It was evident that Mr. Vanderlip had been requested to take this step upon advice of certain members of the Senate committee. Later the truth of this assumption was verified, when the Republican members of the committee reported this plan in modified form to the Senate.

Hearings were closed in October, and the full membership of the Senate committee, both Republicans and Democrats, went into executive session on the bill. In the meantime repeated attempts were made to persuade the President to permit Congress to adjourn and to take up the currency bill at the regular session to meet in December. This the President consistently refused to do. As a consequence the Congress remained technically in session without stop, thereby merging the extra session called in April with the regular session beginning the first Monday in December.

In the meantime the administration bill was by no means having an easy time in committee. Upon the fundamentals the administration Senators were every time outvoted. Senators O'Gorman, of New York; Reed, of Missouri, and Hitchcock, of Nebraska, refused to stand in line with the administration's policies. The President called members of the committee to the White House and lectured them and did everything he could to whip them into line. Finally he had his followers in the Senate call a Democratic conference on the bill, having the statement published that the Democrats could not stand by any report from the committee which failed to receive the support of the majority members.

Upon the day of the conference it was learned that Senators O'Gorman and Reed were back in the Democratic ranks, thereby permitting six Democratic Senators to come together on a bill. Senator Hitchcock still remained recalcitrant. The Democratic conference was dismissed without action and the six Democratic members of the committee left the committee room and began preparing a report on the bill in private. This left Senator Hitchcock and five Republicans in the committee room, who also began the preparation of a separate report to the Senate. On November 20 the two sections of the committee came together and agreed to report a disagreement to the Senate, transmitting two recommendations on the House bill. The report was filed with the Senate two days later.

Immediately plans were drawn for hurried action on the bill. It was desirous that the measure be placed on the statute books before the holiday recess. A Democratic caucus was called which decided to hold the Senate in daily sessions from 10 o'clock in the morning until 11 o'clock at night until a final vote was had on the bill. Furthermore this caucus took up the Democratic draft of the bill, revised it slightly, and endorsed it for Democratic favor.

This action practically assured the passage of the Democratic measure, but the Republican minority in the Senate was able to compel some delay. The minority was successful in keeping up the debate until the week preceding Christmas. This was indeed a task as the Democrats indulged in the debate but sparingly. Finally a vote was taken on the evening of December 19, resulting in a victory for the Democratic measure by a vote of 54 to 34, several Republicans voting with the Democrats.

Plans had been perfected to have but three conferees on the bill from either House, but because this contemplated eliminating his name Senator O'Gorman raised an objection, wherefore the Senate appointed nine conferees, six Democrats and three Republicans. The House appointed three conferees, and the committee began its deliberations on the afternoon of December 20. The conference report was adopted on December 23, and the bill signed by the President on the same day.

Congress immediately adjourned for a rest. This brought to a conclusion possibly the most noted session of Congress during the Wilson administration, a session which placed on the statute books two intensely important measures, a Democratic tariff law and the Federal Reserve Act.

The Federal Reserve Act

Be it enacted by the Senate and House of Representatives of the United States of America in Congress assembled, That the short title of this Act shall be the "Federal Reserve Act."

Wherever the word "bank" is used in this Act, the word shall be held to include State bank, banking association, and trust company, except where national banks or Federal reserve banks are specifically referred to.

The terms "national bank" and "national banking association" used in this Act shall be held to be synonymous and interchangeable. The term "member bank" shall be held to mean any national bank, State bank, or bank or trust company which has become a member of one of the reserve banks created by this Act. The term "board" shall be held to mean Federal Reserve Board; the term "district" shall be held to mean Federal reserve district; the term "reserve bank" shall be held to mean Federal reserve bank.

Federal Reserve Districts

SEC. 2. As soon as practicable, the Secretary of the Treasury, the Secretary of Agriculture and the Comptroller of the Currency, acting as "The Reserve Bank Organization Committee," shall designate not less than eight nor more than twelve cities to be known as Federal reserve cities, and shall divide the continental United States, excluding Alaska, into districts, each district to contain only one of such Federal reserve cities. The determination of said organization committee shall not be subject to review except by the Federal Reserve Board when organized: *Provided,* That the districts shall be apportioned with due regard to the convenience and customary course of business and shall not necessarily be coterminous with any State or States. The districts thus created may be readjusted and new districts may from time to time be created by the Federal Reserve Board, not to exceed twelve in all. Such districts shall be known as Federal reserve districts and may be designated by number. A majority of the organization committee shall constitute a quorum with authority to act.

Said organization committee shall be authorized to employ counsel and expert aid, to take testimony, to send for persons and papers, to administer oaths, and to make such investigation as may be deemed necessary by the said committee in determining the reserve districts and in designating the cities within such districts where such Federal reserve banks shall be severally located. The said committee shall supervise the organization in each of the cities designated of a Federal reserve bank, which shall include in its title the name of the city in which it is situated, as "Federal Reserve Bank of Chicago."

Under regulations to be prescribed by the organization committee, every national banking association in the United States is hereby required, and every eligible bank in the United States and every trust company within the District of Columbia, is hereby authorized to signify in writing, within sixty days after the passage of this Act, its acceptance of the terms and provisions hereof. When the organization committee shall have designated the cities in which Federal reserve banks are to be organized, and fixed the geographical limits of the Federal reserve districts, every national banking association within that district shall be required within thirty days after notice from the organization committee, to subscribe to the capital stock of such Federal reserve bank in a sum equal to six per centum of the paid-up capital stock and surplus of such bank, one-sixth of the subscription to be payable on call of the organization committee or of the Federal Reserve Board, one-sixth within three months and one-sixth within six months thereafter, and the remainder of the subscription, or any part thereof, shall be subject to call when deemed necessary by the Federal

Reserve Board, said payments to be in gold or gold certificates.

The shareholders of every Federal reserve bank shall be held individually responsible, equally and ratably, and not one for another, for all contracts, debts, and engagements of such bank to the extent of the amount of their subscriptions to such stock at the par value thereof in addition to the amount subscribed, whether such subscriptions have been paid up in whole or in part, under the provisions of this Act.

Any national bank failing to signify its acceptance of the terms of this Act within the sixty days aforesaid, shall cease to act as a reserve agent, upon thirty days' notice, to be given within the discretion of the said organization committee or of the Federal Reserve Board.

Should any national banking association in the United States now organized fail within one year after the passage of this Act to become a member bank or fail to comply with any of the provisions of this Act applicable thereto, all of the rights, privileges, and franchises of such association granted to it under the national-bank Act, or under the provisions of this Act, shall be thereby forfeited. Any noncompliance with or violation of this Act shall, however, be determined and adjudged by any court of the United States of competent jurisdiction in a suit brought for that purpose in the District or Territory in which such bank is located, under direction of the Federal Reserve Board, by the Comptroller of the Currency in his own name before the association shall be declared dissolved. In cases of such noncompliance or violation, other than the failure to become a member bank under the provisions of this Act, every director who participated in or assented to the same shall be held liable in his personal or individual capacity for all damages which said bank, its shareholders, or any other person shall have sustained in consequence of such violation.

Such dissolution shall not take away or impair any remedy against such corporation, its stockholders or officers, for any liability or penalty which shall have been previously incurred.

Should the subscriptions by banks to the stock of said Federal reserve banks or any one or more of them be, in the judgment of the organization committee, insufficient to provide the amount of capital required therefor, then and in that event the said organization committee may, under conditions and regulations to be prescribed by it, offer to public subscription at par such an amount of stock in said Federal reserve banks, or any one or more of them, as said committee shall determine, subject to the same conditions as to payment and stock liability as provided for member banks.

No individual, copartnership, or corporation other than a member bank of its district shall be permitted to subscribe for or to hold at any time more than $25,000 par value of stock in any Federal reserve bank. Such stock shall be known as public stock and may be transferred on the books of the Federal reserve bank by the chairman of the board of directors of such bank.

Should the total subscriptions by banks and the public to the stock of said Federal reserve banks, or any one or more of them, be, in the judgment of the organization committee, insufficient to provide the amount of capital required therefor, then and in that event the said organization committee shall allot to the United States such an amount of said stock as said committee shall determine. Said United States stock shall be paid for at par out of any money in the Treasury not otherwise appropriated, and shall be held by the Secretary of the Treasury and disposed of for the benefit of the United States in such manner, at such times, and at such price, not less than par, as the Secretary of the Treasury shall determine.

Stock not held by member banks shall not be entitled to voting power.

The Federal Reserve Board is hereby empowered to adopt and promulgate rules and regulations governing the transfers of said stock.

No Federal reserve bank shall commence business with a subscribed capital less than $4,000,000. The organization of reserve districts and Federal reserve cities shall not be construed as changing the present status of reserve cities and central reserve cities, except in so far as this Act changes the amount of reserves that may be carried with approved reserve agents located therein. The organization committee shall have power to appoint such assistants and incur such expenses in carrying out the provisions of this Act as it shall deem necessary, and such expenses shall be payable by the Treasurer of the United States upon voucher approved by the Secretary of the Treasury, and the sum of $100,000, or so much thereof as may be necessary, is hereby appropriated, out of any moneys in the Treasury not otherwise appropriated, for the payment of such expenses.

Branch Offices

Sec. 3. Each Federal reserve bank shall establish branch banks within the Federal reserve district in which it is located and may do so in the district of any Federal reserve bank which may have been suspended. Such branches shall be operated by a board of directors under rules and regulations approved by the Federal Reserve Board. Directors of branch banks shall possess the same qualifications as directors of the Federal reserve banks. Four of said directors shall be selected by the reserve bank and three by the Federal Reserve Board, and they shall hold office during the pleasure, respectively, of the parent bank and the Federal Reserve Board. The reserve bank shall designate one of the directors as manager.

Federal Reserve Banks

SEC. 4. When the organization committee shall have established Federal reserve districts as provided in section two of this Act, a certificate shall be filed with the Comptroller of the Currency showing the geographical limits of such districts and the Federal reserve city designated in each of such districts. The Comptroller of the Currency shall thereupon cause to be forwarded to each national bank located in each district, and to such other banks declared to be eligible by the organization committee which may apply therefor, an application blank in form to be approved by the organization committee, which blank shall contain a resolution to be adopted by the board of directors of each bank executing such application, authorizing a subscription to the capital stock of the Federal reserve bank organizing in that district in accordance with the provisions of this Act.

When the minimum amount of capital stock prescribed by this Act for the organization of any Federal reserve bank shall have been subscribed and allotted, the organization committee shall designate any five banks of those whose applications have been received, to execute a certificate of organization, and thereupon the banks so designated shall, under their seals, make an organization certificate which shall specifically state the name of such Federal reserve bank, the territorial extent of the district over which the operations of such Federal reserve bank are to be carried on, the city and State in which said bank is to be located, the amount of capital stock and the number of shares into which the same is divided, the name and place of doing business of each bank executing such certificate, and of all banks which have subscribed to the capital stock of such Federal reserve bank and the number of shares subscribed by each, and the fact that the certificate is made to enable those banks executing same, and all banks which have subscribed or may thereafter subscribe to the capital stock of such Federal reserve bank, to avail themselves of the advantages of this Act.

The said organization certificate shall be acknowledged before a judge of some court of record or notary public; and shall be, together with the acknowledgment thereof, authenticated by the seal of such court, or notary, transmitted to the Comptroller of the Currency, who shall file, record and carefully preserve the same in his office.

Upon the filing of such certificate with the Comptroller of the Currency as aforesaid, the said Federal reserve bank shall become a body corporate and as such, and in the name designated in such organization certificate, shall have power—

First. To adopt and use a corporate seal.

Second. To have succession for a period of twenty years from its organization unless it is sooner dissolved by an Act of Congress, or unless its franchise becomes forfeited by some violation of law.

Third. To make contracts.

Fourth. To sue and be sued, complain and defend, in any court of law or equity.

Fifth. To appoint by its board of directors, such officers and employees as are not otherwise provided for in this Act, to define their duties, require bonds of them and fix the penalty thereof, and to dismiss at pleasure such officers or employees.

Sixth. To prescribe by its board of directors, by-laws not inconsistent with law, regulating the manner in which its general business may be conducted, and the privileges granted to it by law may be exercised and enjoyed.

Seventh. To exercise by its board of directors, or duly authorized officers or agents, all powers specifically granted by the provisions of this Act and such incidental powers as shall be necessary to carry on the business of banking within the limitations prescribed by this Act.

Eighth. Upon deposit with the Treasurer of the United States of any bonds of the United States in the manner provided by existing law relating to national banks, to receive from the Comptroller of the Currency circulating notes in blank, registered and countersigned as provided by law, equal in amount to the par value of the bonds so deposited, such notes to be issued under the same conditions and provisions of law as relate to the issue of circulating notes of national banks secured by bonds of the United States bearing the circulating privilege, except that the issue of such notes shall not be limited to the capital stock of such Federal reserve bank.

But no Federal reserve bank shall transact any business except such as is incidental and necessary preliminary to its organization until it has been authorized by the Comptroller of the Currency to commence business under the provisions of this Act.

Every Federal reserve bank shall be conducted under the supervision and control of a board of directors.

The board of directors shall perform the duties usually appertaining to the office of directors of banking associations and all such duties as are prescribed by law.

Said board shall administer the affairs of said bank fairly and impartially and without discrimination in favor of or against any member bank or banks and shall, subject to the provisions of law and the order of the Federal Reserve Board, extend to each member bank such discounts, advancements and accommodations as may be safely and reasonably made with due regard for the claims and demands of other member banks.

Such board of directors shall be selected as hereinafter specified and shall consist of nine members, holding office for three years, and divided into three classes, designated as classes A, B, and C.

Class A shall consist of three members, who shall be chosen by and be representative of the stock-holding banks.

Class B shall consist of three members, who at the time of their election shall be actively engaged in their district in commerce, agriculture or some other industrial pursuit.

Class C shall consist of three members who shall be designated by the Federal Reserve Board. When the necessary subscriptions to the capital stock have been obtained for the organization of any Federal reserve bank, the Federal Reserve Board shall appoint the class C directors and shall designate one of such directors as chairman of the board to be selected. Pending the designation of such chairman, the organization committee shall exercise the powers and duties appertaining to the office of chairman in the organization of such Federal reserve bank.

No Senator or Representative in Congress shall be a member of the Federal Reserve Board or an officer or a director of a Federal reserve bank.

No director of class B shall be an officer, director, or employee of any bank.

No director of class C shall be an officer, director, employee, or stockholder of any bank.

Directors of class A and class B shall be chosen in the following manner:

The chairman of the board of directors of the Federal reserve bank of the district in which the bank is situated or, pending the appointment of such chairman, the organization committee shall classify the member banks of the district into three general groups or divisions. Each group shall contain as nearly as may be one-third of the aggregate number of the member banks of the district and shall consist, as nearly as may be, of banks of similar capitalization. The groups shall be designated by number by the chairman.

At a regularly called meeting of the board of directors of each member bank in the district it shall elect by ballot a district reserve elector and shall certify his name to the chairman of the board of directors of the Federal reserve bank of the district. The chairman shall make lists of the district reserve electors thus named by banks in each of the aforesaid three groups and shall transmit one list to each elector in each group.

Each member bank shall be permitted to nominate to the chairman one candidate for director of class A and one candidate for director of class B. The candidates so nominated shall be listed by the chairman, indicating by whom nominated, and a copy of said list shall, within fifteen days after its completion, be furnished by the chairman to each elector.

Every elector shall, within fifteen days after the receipt of the said list, certify to the chairman his first, second and other choices of a director of class A and class B, respectively, upon a preferential ballot, on a form furnished by the chairman of the board of directors of the Federal reserve bank of the district. Each elector shall make a cross opposite the name of the first, second and other choices for a director of class A and for a director of class B, but shall not vote more than one choice for any one candidate.

Any candidate having a majority of all votes cast in the column of first choice shall be declared elected. If no candidate have a majority of all the votes in the first column, then there shall be added together the votes cast by the electors for such candidates in the second column and the votes cast for the several candidates in the first column. If any candidate then have a majority of the electors voting, by adding together the first and second choices, he shall be declared elected. If no candidate have a majority of electors voting when the first and second choices shall have been added, then the votes cast in the third column for other choices shall be added together in like manner, and the candidate then having the highest number of votes shall be declared elected. An immediate report of election shall be declared.

Class C directors shall be appointed by the Federal Reserve Board. They shall have been for at least two years residents of the district for which they are appointed, one of whom shall be designated by said board as chairman of the board of directors of the Federal reserve bank and as "Federal reserve agent." He shall be a person of tested banking experience; and in addition to his duties as chairman of the board of directors of the Federal reserve bank he shall be required to maintain, under regulations to be established by the Federal Reserve Board a local office of said board on the premises of the Federal reserve bank. He shall make regular reports to the Federal Reserve Board, and shall act as its official representative for the performance of the functions conferred upon it by this Act. He shall receive an annual compensation to be fixed by the Federal Reserve Board and paid monthly by the Federal reserve bank to which he is designated. One of the directors of class C, who shall be a person of tested banking experience, shall be appointed by the Federal Reserve

Board as deputy chairman and deputy Federal reserve agent to exercise the powers of the chairman of the board and Federal reserve agent in case of absence or disability of his principal.

Directors of Federal reserve banks shall receive, in addition to any compensation otherwise provided, a reasonable allowance for necessary expenses in attending meetings of their respective boards, which amount shall be paid by the respective Federal reserve banks. Any compensation that may be provided by boards of directors of Federal reserve banks for directors, officers or employees shall be subject to the approval of the Federal Reserve Board.

The Reserve Bank Organization Committee may, in organizing Federal reserve banks, call such meetings of bank directors in the several districts as may be necessary to carry out the purposes of this Act, and may exercise the functions herein conferred upon the chairman of the board of directors of each Federal reserve bank pending the complete organization of such bank.

At the first meeting of the full board of directors of each Federal reserve bank, it shall be the duty of the directors of classes A, B and C, respectively, to designate one of the members of each class whose term of office shall expire in one year from the first of January nearest to date of such meeting, one whose term of office shall expire at the end of two years from said date, and one whose term of office shall expire at the end of three years from said date. Thereafter every director of a Federal reserve bank chosen as hereinbefore provided shall hold office for a term of three years. Vacancies that may occur in the several classes of directors of Federal reserve banks may be filled in the manner provided for the original selection of such directors, such appointees to hold office for the unexpired terms of their predecessors.

Stock Issues—Increase & Decrease of Capital

SEC. 5. The capital stock of each Federal reserve bank shall be divided into shares of $100 each. The outstanding capital stock shall be increased from time to time as member banks increase their capital stock and surplus or as additional banks become members, and may be decreased as member banks reduce their capital stock or surplus or cease to be members. Shares of the capital stock of Federal reserve banks owned by member banks shall not be transferred or hypothecated. When a member bank increases its capital stock or surplus, it shall thereupon subscribe for an additional amount of capital stock of the Federal reserve bank of its district equal to six per centum of the said increase, one-half of said subscription to be paid in the manner hereinbefore provided for original subscription and one-half subject to call of the Federal Reserve Board. A bank applying for stock in a Federal reserve bank at any time after the organization thereof must subscribe for an amount of the capital stock of the Federal reserve bank equal to six per centum of the paid-up capital stock and surplus of said applicant bank, paying therefor its par value plus one-half of one per centum a month from the period of the last dividend. When the capital stock of any Federal reserve bank shall have been increased, either on account of the increase of capital stock of member banks or on account of the increase in the number of member banks, the board of directors shall cause to be executed a certificate to the Comptroller of the Currency showing the increase in capital stock, the amount paid in, and by whom paid. When a member bank reduces its capital stock it shall surrender a proportionate amount of its holdings in the capital of said Federal reserve bank, and when a member bank voluntarily liquidates it shall surrender all of its holdings of the capital stock of said Federal reserve bank and be released from its stock subscription not previously called. In either case the shares surrendered shall be canceled and the member bank shall receive in payment therefor, under regulations to be prescribed by the Federal Reserve

Board, a sum equal to its cash-paid subscriptions on the shares surrendered and one-half of one per centum a month from the period of the last dividend, not to exceed the book value thereof, less any liability of such member bank to the Federal reserve bank.

Sec. 6. If any member bank shall be declared insolvent and a receiver appointed therefor, the stock held by it in said Federal reserve bank shall be canceled, without impairment of its liability, and all cash-paid subscriptions on said stock, with one-half of one per centum per month from the period of last dividend, not to exceed the book value thereof, shall be first applied to all debts of the insolvent member bank to the Federal reserve bank, and the balance, if any, shall be paid to the receiver of the insolvent bank. Whenever the capital stock of a Federal reserve bank is reduced, either on account of a reduction in capital stock of any member bank or of the liquidation or insolvency of such bank, the board of directors shall cause to be executed a certificate to the Comptroller of the Currency showing such reduction of capital stock and the amount repaid to such bank.

Division of Earnings

Sec. 7. After all necessary expenses of a Federal reserve bank have been paid or provided for, the stockholders shall be entitled to receive an annual dividend of six per centum on the paid-in capital stock, which dividend shall be cumulative. After the aforesaid dividend claims have been fully met, all the net earnings shall be paid to the United States as a franchise tax, except that one-half of such net earnings shall be paid into a surplus fund until it shall amount to forty per centum of the paid-in capital stock of such bank.

The net earnings derived by the United States from Federal reserve banks shall, in the discretion of the Secretary, be used to supplement the gold reserve held against outstanding United States notes, or shall be applied to the reduction of the outstanding bonded indebtedness of the United States under regulations to be prescribed by the Secretary of the Treasury. Should a Federal reserve bank be dissolved or go into liquidation, any surplus remaining, after the payment of all debts, dividend requirements as hereinbefore provided, and the par value of the stock, shall be paid to and become the property of the United States and shall be similarly applied.

Federal reserve banks, including the capital stock and surplus therein and the income derived therefrom, shall be exempt from Federal, State, and local taxation, except taxes upon real estate.

SEC. 8. Section fifty-one hundred and fifty-four, United States Revised Statutes, is hereby amended to read as follows:

Any bank incorporated by special law of any State or of the United States or organized under the general laws of any State or of the United States and having an unimpaired capital sufficient to entitle it to become a national banking association under the provisions of the existing laws may, by the vote of the shareholders owning not less than fifty-one per centum of the capital stock of such bank or banking association, with the approval of the Comptroller of the Currency, be converted into a national banking association, with any name approved by the Comptroller of the Currency: *Provided, however,* That said conversion shall not be in contravention of the State law. . In such case the articles of association and organization certificate may be executed by a majority of the directors of the bank or banking institution, and the certificate shall declare that the owners of fifty-one per centum of the capital stock have authorized the directors to make such certificate and to change or convert the bank or banking institution into a national association. A majority of the directors, after executing the articles of association and the organization certificate, shall have power to execute all other papers and to do whatever may be required to make its organization perfect and complete as a national association. The shares of any such bank may continue to be for the same amount each as they were before the conversion, and the directors may continue to be directors of the association until others are elected or appointed in accordance with the provisions of the statutes of the United States. When the comptroller has given to such bank or banking association a certificate that the provisions of this Act have been complied with, such bank or banking association, and all its stockholders, officers, and employees, shall have the same powers and privileges, and shall be subject to the same duties, liabilities, and regulations, in all respects, as shall have been prescribed by the Federal Reserve Act and by the national banking Act for associations originally organized as national banking associations.

State Banks as Members

SEC. 9. Any bank incorporated by special law of any State, or organized under the general laws of any State or of the United States, may make application to the reserve bank organization committee, pending organization, and thereafter to the Federal Reserve Board for the right to subscribe to the stock of the Federal reserve bank organized or to be organized within the Federal reserve district where the applicant is located. The organization committee or the Federal Reserve Board, under such rules and regulations as it may prescribe, subject to the provisions of this section, may permit the applying bank to become a stockholder in the Federal reserve bank of the district in which the applying bank is located. Whenever the organization committee or the Federal Reserve Board shall permit the applying bank to become a stockholder in the Federal reserve bank of the district, stock shall be issued and paid for under the rules and regulations in this Act provided for national banks which become stockholders in Federal reserve banks.

The organization committee or the Federal Reserve Board shall establish by-laws for the general government of its conduct in acting upon applications made by the State banks and banking associations and trust companies for stock ownership in Federal reserve banks. Such by-laws shall require applying banks not organized under Federal law to comply with the reserve and capital requirements and to submit to the examination and regulations prescribed by the organization committee or by the Federal Reserve Board. No applying bank shall be admitted to membership in a Federal reserve bank unless it possesses a paid-up unimpaired capital sufficient to entitle it to become a national banking association in the place where it is situated, under the provisions of the national banking Act.

Any bank becoming a member of a Federal reserve bank under the provisions of this section shall, in addition to the regulations and restrictions hereinbefore provided, be required to conform to the provisions of law imposed on the national banks respecting the limitation of liability which may be incurred by any person, firm, or corporation to such banks, the prohibition against making purchase of or loans on stock of such banks, and the withdrawal or impairment of capital, or the payment of unearned dividends, and to such rules and regulations as the Federal Reserve Board may, in pursuance thereof, prescribe.

Such banks, and the officers, agents, and employees thereof, shall also be subject to the provisions of and to the penalties prescribed by sections fifty-one hundred and ninety-eight, fifty-two hundred, fifty-two hundred and one, and fifty-two hundred and eight, and fifty-two hundred and nine of the Revised Statutes. The member banks shall also be required to make reports of the conditions and of the payments of dividends to the comptroller, as provided in sections fifty-two hundred and eleven and fifty-two hundred and twelve of the Revised

Statutes, and shall be subject to the penalties prescribed by section fifty-two hundred and thirteen for the failure to make such report.

If at any time it shall appear to the Federal Reserve Board that a member bank has failed to comply with the provisions of this section or the regulations of the Federal Reserve Board, it shall be within the power of the said board, after hearing, to require such bank to surrender its stock in the Federal reserve bank; upon such surrender the Federal reserve bank shall pay the cash-paid subscriptions to the said stock with interest at the rate of one-half of one per centum per month, computed from the last dividend, if earned, not to exceed the book value thereof, less any liability to said Federal reserve bank, except the subscription liability not previously called, which shall be canceled, and said Federal reserve bank shall, upon notice from the Federal Reserve Board, be required to suspend said bank from further privileges of membership, and shall within thirty days of such notice cancel and retire its stock and make payment therefor in the manner herein provided.

The Federal Reserve Board may restore membership upon due proof of compliance with the conditions imposed by this section.

Federal Reserve Board

SEC. 10. A Federal Reserve Board is hereby created which shall consist of seven members, including the Secretary of the Treasury and the Comptroller of the Currency, who shall be members ex-officio, and five members appointed by the President of the United States, by and with the advice and consent of the Senate. In selecting the five appointive members of the Federal Reserve Board, not more than one of whom shall be selected from any one Federal reserve district, the President shall have due regard to a fair representation of the different commercial, industrial and geographical divisions of the country. The five members of the Federal Reserve Board appointed by the President and confirmed as aforesaid shall devote their entire time to the business of the Federal Reserve Board and shall each receive an annual salary of $12,000, payable monthly together with actual necessary traveling expenses, and the Comptroller of the Currency, as ex-officio member of the Federal Reserve Board, shall, in addition to the salary now paid him as Comptroller of the Currency, receive the sum of $7,000 annually for his services as a member of said Board.

The members of said board, the Secretary of the Treasury, the Assistant Secretaries of the Treasury, and the Comptroller of the Currency shall be ineligible during the time they are in office and for two years thereafter to hold any office, position, or employment in any member bank. Of the five members thus appointed by the President at least two shall be persons experienced in banking or finance. One shall be designated by the President to serve for two, one for four, one for six, one for eight, and one for ten years, and thereafter each member so appointed shall serve for a term of ten years unless sooner removed for cause by the President. Of the five persons thus appointed, one shall be designated by the President as governor and one as vice-governor of the Federal Reserve Board. The governor of the Federal Reserve Board, subject to its supervision, shall be the active executive officer. The Secretary of the Treasury may assign offices in the Department of the Treasury for the use of the Federal Reserve Board. Each member of the Federal Reserve Board shall within fifteen days after notice of appointment make and subscribe to the oath of office.

The Federal Reserve Board shall have power to levy semi-annually upon the Federal reserve banks, in proportion to their capital stock and surplus, an assessment sufficient to pay its estimated expenses and the salaries of its members and employees for the half year succeeding the levying of such assessment, together with any deficit carried forward from the preceding half year.

The first meeting of the Federal Reserve Board shall be held in Washington, District of Columbia, as soon as may be after the passage of this Act, at a date to be fixed by the Reserve Bank Organization Committee. The Secretary of the Treasury shall be ex-officio chairman of the Federal Reserve Board. No member of the Federal Reserve Board shall be an officer or director of any bank, banking institution, trust company, or Federal reserve bank nor hold stock in any bank, banking institution, or trust company; and before entering upon his duties as a member of the Federal Reserve Board he shall certify under oath to the Secretary of the Treasury that he has complied with this requirement. Whenever a vacancy shall occur, other than by expiration of term, among the five members of the Federal Reserve Board appointed by the President, as above provided, a successor shall be appointed by the President, with the advice and consent of the Senate, to fill such vacancy, and when appointed he shall hold office for the unexpired term of the member whose place he is selected to fill.

The President shall have power to fill all vacancies that may happen on the Federal Reserve Board during the recess of the Senate, by granting commissions which shall expire thirty days after the next session of the Senate convenes.

Nothing in this Act contained shall be construed as taking away any powers heretofore vested by law in the Secretary of the Treasury which relate to the supervision, management, and control of the Treasury Department and bureaus under such department, and wherever any power vested by this Act in the Federal Reserve Board or the Federal reserve agent appears to conflict with the powers of the Secretary of the Treasury, such powers shall be exercised subject to the supervision and control of the Secretary.

The Federal Reserve Board shall annually make a full report of its operations to the Speaker of the House of Representatives, who shall cause the same to be printed for the information of the Congress.

Section three hundred and twenty-four of the Revised Statutes of the United States shall be amended so as to read as follows: There shall be in the Department of the Treasury a bureau charged with the execution of all laws passed by Congress relating to the issue and regulation of national currency secured by United States bonds and, under the general supervision of the Federal Reserve Board, of all Federal reserve notes, the chief officer of which bureau shall be called the Comptroller of the Currency and shall perform his duties under the general directions of the Secretary of the Treasury.

SEC. 11. The Federal Reserve Board shall be authorized and empowered:

(a) To examine at its discretion the accounts, books and affairs of each Federal reserve bank and of each member bank and to require such statements and reports as it may deem necessary. The said board shall publish once each week a statement showing the condition of each Federal reserve bank and a consolidated statement for all Federal reserve banks. Such statements shall show in detail the assets and liabilities of the Federal reserve banks, single and combined, and shall furnish full information regarding the character of the money held as reserve and the amount, nature and maturities of the paper and other investments owned or held by Federal reserve banks.

(b) To permit, or, on the affirmative vote of at least five members of the Reserve Board, to require Federal reserve banks to rediscount the discounted paper of other Federal reserve banks at rates of interest to be fixed by the Federal Reserve Board.

(c)   To suspend for a period not exceeding thirty days, and from time to time to renew such suspension for periods not exceeding fifteen days, any reserve requirement specified in this Act: *Provided,* That it shall establish a graduated tax upon the amounts by which the reserve requirements of this Act may be permitted to fall below the level hereinafter specified: *And provided further,* That when the gold reserve held against Federal reserve notes falls below forty per centum, the Federal Reserve Board shall establish a graduated tax of not more than one per centum per annum upon such deficiency until the reserves fall to thirty-two and one-half per centum, and when said reserve falls below thirty-two and one-half per centum, a tax at the rate increasingly of not less than one and one-half per centum per annum upon each two and one-half per centum or fraction thereof that such reserve falls below thirty-two and one-half per centum. The tax shall be paid by the reserve bank, but the reserve bank shall add an amount equal to said tax to the rates of interest and discount fixed by the Federal Reserve Board.

(d)   To supervise and regulate through the bureau under the charge of the Comptroller of the Currency the issue and retirement of Federal reserve notes, and to prescribe rules and regulations under which such notes may be delivered by the Comptroller to the Federal reserve agents applying therefor.

(e)   To add to the number of cities classified as reserve and central reserve cities under existing law in which national banking associations are subject to the reserve requirements set forth in section twenty of this Act; or to reclassify existing reserve and central reserve cities or to terminate their designation as such.

(f)   To suspend or remove any officer or director of any Federal reserve bank, the cause of such removal to be forthwith communicated in writing by the Federal Reserve Board to the removed officer or director and to said bank.

(g)   To require the writing off of doubtful or worthless assets upon the books and balance sheets of Federal reserve banks.

(h)   To suspend, for the violation of any of the provisions of this Act, the operations of any Federal reserve bank, to take possession thereof, administer the same during the period of suspension, and, when deemed advisable, to liquidate or reorganize such bank.

(i)   To require bonds of Federal reserve agents, to make regulations for the safeguarding of all collateral, bonds, Federal reserve notes, money or property of any kind deposited in the hands of such agents, and said board shall perform the duties, functions, or services specified in this Act, and make all rules and regulations necessary to enable said board effectively to perform the same.

(j) To exercise general supervision over said Federal reserve banks.

(k) To grant by special permit to national banks applying therefor, when not in contravention of State or local law, the right to act as trustee, executor, administrator, or registrar of stocks and bonds under such rules and regulations as the said board may prescribe.

(l) To employ such attorneys, experts, assistants, clerks, or other employees as may be deemed necessary to conduct the business of the board. All salaries and fees shall be fixed in advance by said board and shall be paid in the same manner as the salaries of the members of said board. All such attorneys, experts, assistants, clerks, and other employees shall be appointed without regard to the provisions of the Act of January sixteenth, eighteen hundred and eighty-three (volume twenty-two, United States Statutes at Large, page four hundred and three), and amendments thereto, or any rule or regulation made in pursuance thereof: *Provided*, That nothing herein shall prevent the President from placing said employees in the classified service.

Federal Advisory Council

SEC. 12. There is hereby created a Federal Advisory Council, which shall consist of as many members as there are Federal reserve districts. Each Federal reserve bank by its board of directors shall annually select from its own Federal reserve district one member of said council, who shall receive such compensation and allowances as may be fixed by his board of directors subject to the approval of the Federal Reserve Board. The meetings of said advisory council shall be held at Washington, District of Columbia, at least four times each year, and oftener if called by the Federal Reserve Board. The council may, in addition to the meetings above provided for, hold such other meetings in Washington, District of Columbia, or elsewhere, as it may deem necessary, may select its own officers and adopt its own methods of procedure, and a majority of its members shall constitute a quorum for the transaction of business. Vacancies in the council shall be filled by the respective reserve banks, and members selected to fill vacancies shall serve for the unexpired term.

The Federal Advisory Council shall have power, by itself or through its officers, (1) to confer directly with the Federal Reserve Board on general business conditions; (2) to make oral or written representations concerning matters within the jurisdiction of said board; (3) to call for information and to make recommendations in regard to discount rates, rediscount business, note issues, reserve conditions in the various districts, the purchase and sale of gold or securities by reserve banks, open-market operations by said banks, and the general affairs of the reserve banking system.

Powers of Federal Reserve Banks

Sec. 13. Any Federal reserve bank may receive from any of its member banks, and from the United States, deposits of current funds in lawful money, national-bank notes, Federal reserve notes, or checks and drafts upon solvent member banks, payable upon presentation; or, solely for exchange purposes, may receive from other Federal reserve banks deposits of current funds in lawful money, national-bank notes, or checks and drafts upon solvent members of other Federal reserve banks, payable upon presentation.

Upon the indorsement of any of its member banks, with a waiver of demand, notice and protest by such bank, any Federal reserve bank may discount notes, drafts, and bills of exchange arising out of actual commericial transactions; that is, notes, drafts, and bills of exchange issued or drawn for agricultural, industrial, or commercial purposes, or the proceeds of which have been used, or are to be used, for such purposes, the Federal Reserve Board to have the right to determine or define the character of the paper thus eligible for discount, within the meaning of this Act. Nothing in this Act contained shall be construed to prohibit such notes, drafts, and bills of exchange, secured by staple agricultural products, or other goods, wares, or merchandise from being eligible for such discount; but such definition shall not include notes, drafts, or bills covering merely investments or issued or drawn for the purpose of carrying or trading in stocks, bonds, or other investment securities, except bonds and notes of the Government of the United States. Notes, drafts, and bills admitted to discount under the terms of this paragraph must have a maturity at the time of discount, of not more than ninety days: *Provided,* That notes, drafts, and bills drawn or issued for agricultural purposes or based on live stock and having a maturity not exceeding six months may be discounted in an amount to be limited to a percentage of the capital of the Federal reserve bank, to be ascertained and fixed by the Federal Reserve Board.

Any Federal reserve bank may discount acceptances which are based on the importation or exportation of goods and which have a maturity at time of discount of not more than three months, and indorsed by at least one member bank. The amount of acceptances so discounted shall at no time exceed one-half the paid-up capital stock and surplus of the bank for which the rediscounts are made.

The aggregate of such notes and bills bearing the signature or indorsement of any one person, company, firm, or corporation rediscounted for any one bank shall at no time exceed ten per centum of the unimpaired capital and surplus of said bank; but this restriction shall not apply to the discount of bills of exchange drawn in good faith against actually existing values.

Any member bank may accept drafts or bills of exchange drawn upon it and growing out of transactions involving the importation or exportation of goods having not more than six months sight to run; but no bank shall accept such bills to an amount equal at any time in the aggregate to more than one-half its paid-up capital stock and surplus.

Section fifty-two hundred and two of the Revised Statutes of the United States is hereby amended so as to read as follows: No national banking association shall at any time be indebted, or in any way liable, to an amount exceeding the amount of its capital stock at such time actually paid in and remaining undiminished by losses or otherwise, except on account of demands of the nature following:

First. Notes of circulation.

Second. Moneys deposited with or collected by the association.

Third. Bills of exchange or drafts drawn against money actually on deposit to the credit of the association, or due thereto.

Fourth. Liabilities to the stockholders of the association for dividends and reserve profits.

Fifth. Liabilities incurred under the provisions of the Federal Reserve Act.

The rediscount by any Federal reserve bank of any bills receivable and of domestic and foreign bills of exchange, and of acceptances authorized by this Act, shall be subject to such restrictions, limitations, and regulations as may be imposed by the Federal Reserve Board.

Open Market Operations

Sec. 14. Any Federal reserve bank may, under rules and regulations prescribed by the Federal Reserve Board, purchase and sell in the open market, at home or abroad, either from or to domestic or foreign banks, firms, corporations, or individuals, cable transfers and bankers' acceptances and bills of exchange of the kinds and maturities by this Act made eligible for rediscount, with or without the indorsement of a member bank.

Every Federal reserve bank shall have power:

(a) To deal in gold coin and bullion at home or abroad, to make loans thereon, exchange Federal reserve notes for gold, gold coin, or gold certificates, and to contract for loans of gold coin or bullion, giving therefor, when necessary, acceptable security, including the hypothecation of United States bonds or other securities which Federal reserve banks are authorized to hold;

(b) To buy and sell, at home or abroad, bonds and notes of the United States, and bills, notes, revenue bonds, and warrants with a maturity from date of purchase of not exceeding six months, issued in anticipation of the collection of taxes or in anticipation of the receipt of assured revenues by any State, county, district, political subdivision, or municipality in the continental districts, such purchases to be made in accordance with rules and regulations prescribed by the Federal Reserve Board;

(c) To purchase from member banks and to sell, with or without its indorsement, bills of exchange arising out of commercial transactions, as hereinbefore defined:

(d) To establish from time to time, subject to review and determination of the Federal Reserve Board, rates of discount to be charged by the Federal reserve bank for each class of paper, which shall be fixed with a view of accommodating commerce and business;

(e) To establish accounts with other Federal reserve banks for exchange purposes and, with the consent of the Federal Reserve Board, to open and maintain banking accounts in foreign countries, appoint correspondents, and establish agencies in such countries wheresoever it may deem best for the purpose of purchasing, selling, and collecting bills of exchange, and to buy and sell, with or without its indorsement, through such correspondents or agencies, bills of exchange arising out of actual commercial transactions which have not more than ninety days to run and which bear the signature of two or more responsible parties.

Government Deposits

SEC. 15. The moneys held in the general fund of the Treasury, except the five per centum fund for the redemption of outstanding national-bank notes and the funds provided in this Act for the redemption of Federal reserve notes, may, upon the direction of the Secretary of the Treasury, be deposited in Federal reserve banks, which banks, when required by the Secretary of the Treasury, shall act as fiscal agents of the United States; and the revenues of the Government or any part thereof may be deposited in such banks, and disbursements may be made by checks drawn against such deposits.

No public funds of the Philippine Islands, or of the postal savings, or any Government funds, shall be deposited in the continental United States in any bank not belonging to the system established by this Act: *Provided, however,* That nothing in this Act shall be construed to deny the right of the Secretary of the Treasury to use member banks as depositories.

Note Issues

SEC. 16. Federal reserve notes, to be issued at the discretion of the Federal Reserve Board for the purpose of making advances to Federal reserve banks through the Federal reserve agents as hereinafter set forth and for no other purpose, are hereby authorized. The said notes shall be obligations of the United States and shall be receivable by all national and member banks and Federal reserve banks and for all taxes, customs, and other public dues. They shall be redeemed in gold on demand at the Treasury Department of the United States, in the city of Washington, District of Columbia, or in gold or lawful money at any Federal reserve bank.

Any Federal reserve bank may make application to the local Federal reserve agent for such amount of the Federal reserve notes hereinbefore provided for as it may require. Such application shall be accompanied with a tender to the local Federal reserve agent of collateral in amount equal to the sum of the Federal reserve notes thus applied for and issued pursuant to such application. The collateral security thus offered shall be notes and bills, accepted for rediscount under the provisions of section thirteen of this Act, and the Federal reserve agent shall each day notify the Federal Reserve Board of all issues and withdrawals of Federal reserve notes to and by the Federal reserve bank to which he is accredited. The said Federal Reserve Board may at any time call upon a Federal reserve bank for additional security to protect the Federal reserve notes issued to it.

Every Federal reserve bank shall maintain reserves in gold or lawful money of not less than thirty-five per centum against its deposits and reserves in gold of not less than forty per centum against its Federal reserve notes in actual circulation, and not offset by gold or lawful money deposited with the Federal reserve agent. Notes so paid out shall bear upon their faces a distinctive letter and serial number, which shall be assigned by the Federal Reserve Board to each Federal reserve bank. Whenever Federal reserve notes issued through one Federal reserve bank shall be received by another Federal reserve bank they shall be promptly returned for credit or redemption to the Federal reserve bank through which they were originally issued. No Federal reserve bank shall pay out notes issued through another under penalty of a tax of ten per centum upon the face value of notes so paid out. Notes presented for redemption at the Treasury of the United States shall be paid out of the redemption fund and returned to the Federal reserve banks through which they were originally issued, and thereupon such Federal reserve bank shall, upon demand of the Secretary of the Treasury, reimburse such redemption fund in lawful money, or, if such Federal reserve notes have been redeemed by the Treasurer in gold or gold certificates, then such funds shall be reimbursed to the extent deemed necessary by the Secretary of the Treasury in gold or gold certificates, and such Federal reserve bank shall, so long as any of its Federal reserve notes remain outstanding, maintain with the Treasurer in gold an amount sufficient in the judgment of the Secretary to provide for all redemptions to be made by the Treasurer. Federal reserve notes received by the Treasury, otherwise than for redemption, may be exchanged for gold out of the redemption fund hereinafter provided and returned to the reserve bank through which they were originally issued, or they may be returned to such bank for the credit of the United States. Federal reserve notes unfit for circulation shall be returned by the Federal reserve agents to the Comptroller of the Currency for cancellation and destruction.

The Federal Reserve Board shall require each Federal reserve bank to maintain on deposit in the Treasury of the United States a sum in gold sufficient in the judgment of the Secretary of the Treasury for the redemption of the Federal reserve notes issued to such bank, but in no event less than five per centum; but such deposit of gold shall be counted and included as part of the forty per centum reserve hereinbefore required. The board shall have the right, acting through the Federal reserve agent, to grant in whole or in part or to reject entirely the application of any Federal reserve bank for Federal reserve notes; but to the extent that such application may be granted the Federal Reserve Board shall, through its local Federal reserve agent, supply Federal reserve notes to the bank so applying, and such bank shall be charged with the amount of such notes and shall pay such rate of interest on said amount as may be established by the Federal Reserve Board, and the amount of such Federal reserve notes so issued to any such bank shall, upon delivery, together with such notes of such Federal reserve bank as may be issued under section eighteen of this Act upon security of United States two per centum Government bonds, become a first and paramount lien on all the assets of such bank.

Any Federal reserve bank may at any time reduce its liability for outstanding Federal reserve notes by depositing, with the Federal reserve agent, its Federal reserve notes, gold, gold certificates, or lawful money of the United States. Federal reserve notes so deposited shall not be reissued, except upon compliance with the conditions of an original issue.

The Federal reserve agent shall hold such gold, gold certificates, or lawful money available exclusively for exchange for the outstanding Federal reserve notes when offered by the reserve bank of which he is a director. Upon the request of the Secretary of the Treasury the Federal Reserve Board shall require the Federal reserve agent to transmit so much of said gold to the Treasury of the United States as may be required for the exclusive purpose of the redemption of such notes.

Any Federal reserve bank may at its discretion withdraw collateral deposited with the local Federal reserve agent for the protection of its Federal reserve notes deposited with it and shall at the same time substitute therefor other like collateral of equal amount with the approval of the Federal reserve agent under regulations to be prescribed by the Federal Reserve Board.

In order to furnish suitable notes for circulation as Federal reserve notes, the Comptroller of the Currency shall, under the direction of the Secretary of the Treasury, cause plates and dies to be engraved in the best manner to guard against counterfeits and fraudulent alterations, and shall have printed therefrom and numbered such quantities of such notes of the denominations of $5, $10, $20, $50, $100, as may be required to supply the Federal reserve banks. Such notes shall be in form and tenor as directed by the Secretary of the Treasury under the provisions of this Act and shall bear the distinctive numbers of the several Federal reserve banks through which they are issued.

When such notes have been prepared, they shall be deposited in the Treasury, or in the subtreasury or mint of the United States nearest the place of business of each Federal reserve bank and shall be held for the use of such bank subject to the order of the Comptroller of the Currency for their delivery, as provided by this Act.

The plates and dies to be procured by the Comptroller of the Currency for the printing of such circulating notes shall remain under his control and direction, and the expenses necessarily incurred in executing the laws relating to the procuring of such notes, and all other expenses incidental to their issue and retirement, shall be paid by the Federal reserve banks, and the Federal Reserve Board shall include in its estimate of expenses levied against the Federal reserve banks a sufficient amount to cover the expenses herein provided for.

The examination of plates, dies, bed pieces, and so forth, and regulations relating to such examination of plates, dies, and so forth, of national-bank notes provided for in section fifty-one hundred and seventy-four Revised Statutes, is hereby extended to include notes herein provided for.

The Federal Reserve Act

Any appropriation heretofore made out of the general funds of the Treasury for engraving plates and dies, the purchase of distinctive paper, or to cover any other expense in connection with the printing of national-bank notes or notes provided for by the Act of May thirtieth, nineteen hundred and eight, and any distinctive paper that may be on hand at the time of the passage of this Act may be used in the discretion of the Secretary for the purposes of this Act, and should the appropriations heretofore made be insufficient to meet the requirements of this Act in addition to circulating notes provided for by existing law, the Secretary is hereby authorized to use so much of any funds in the Treasury not otherwise appropriated for the purpose of furnishing the notes aforesaid: *Provided, however,* That nothing in this section contained shall be construed as exempting national banks or Federal reserve banks from their liability to reimburse the United States for any expenses incurred in printing and issuing circulating notes.

Every Federal reserve bank shall receive on deposit at par from member banks or from Federal reserve banks checks and drafts drawn upon any of its depositors, and when remitted by a Federal reserve bank, checks and drafts drawn by any depositor in any other Federal reserve bank or member bank upon funds to the credit of said depositor in said reserve bank or member bank. Nothing herein contained shall be construed as prohibiting a member bank from charging its actual expense incurred in collecting and remitting funds, or for exchange sold to its patrons. The Federal Reserve Board shall, by rule, fix the charges to be collected by the member banks from its patrons whose checks are cleared through the Federal reserve bank and the charge which may be imposed for the service of clearing or collection rendered by the Federal reserve bank.

The Federal Reserve Board shall make and promulgate from time to time regulations governing the transfer of funds and charges therefor among Federal reserve banks and their branches, and may at its discretion exercise the functions of a clearing house for such Federal reserve banks, or may designate a Federal reserve bank to exercise such functions, and may also require each such bank to exercise the functions of a clearing house for its member banks.

SEC. 17. So much of the provisions of section fifty-one hundred and fifty-nine of the Revised Statutes of the United States, and section four of the Act of June twentieth, eighteen hundred and seventy-four, and section eight of the Act of July twelfth, eighteen hundred and eighty-two, and of any other provisions of existing statutes as require that, before any national banking association shall be authorized to commence banking business, it shall transfer and deliver to the Treasurer of the United States a stated amount of United States registered bonds is hereby repealed.

Refunding Bonds

SEC. 18. After two years from the passage of this Act, and at any time during a period of twenty years thereafter, any member bank desiring to retire the whole or any part of its circulating notes, may file with the Treasurer of the United States an application to sell for its account, at par and accrued interest, United States bonds securing circulation to be retired.

The Treasurer shall, at the end of each quarterly period, furnish the Federal Reserve Board with a list of such applications, and the Federal Reserve Board may, in its discretion, require the Federal reserve banks to purchase such bonds from the banks whose applications have been filed with the Treasurer at least ten days before the end of any quarterly period at which the Federal Reserve Board may direct the purchase to be made: *Provided,* That Federal reserve banks shall not be permitted to purchase an amount to exceed $25,000,-000 of such bonds in any one year, and which amount shall include bonds acquired under section four of this Act by the Federal reserve bank. *Provided further,* That the Federal Reserve Board shall allot to each Federal reserve bank such proportion of such bonds as the capital and surplus of such bank shall bear to the aggregate capital and surplus of all the Federal reserve banks.

Upon notice from the Treasurer of the amount of bonds so sold for its account, each member bank shall duly assign and transfer, in writing, such bonds to the Federal reserve bank purchasing the same, and such Federal reserve bank shall, thereupon, deposit lawful money with the Treasurer of the United States for the purchase price of such bonds, and the Treasurer shall pay to the member bank selling such bonds any balance due after deducting a sufficient sum to redeem its outstanding notes secured by such bonds, which notes shall be canceled and permanently retired when redeemed.

The Federal reserve banks purchasing such bonds shall be permitted to take out an amount of circulating notes equal to the par value of such bonds.

Upon the deposit with the Treasurer of the United States of bonds so purchased, or any bonds with the circulating privilege acquired under section four of this

Act, any Federal reserve bank making such deposit in the manner provided by existing law, shall be entitled to receive from the Comptroller of the Currency circulating notes in blank, registered and countersigned as provided by law, equal in amount to the par value of the bonds so deposited. Such notes shall be the obligations of the Federal reserve bank procuring the same, and shall be in form prescribed by the Secretary of the Treasury, and to the same tenor and effect as national-bank notes now provided by law. They shall be issued and redeemed under the same terms and conditions as national-bank notes except that they shall not be limited to the amount of the capital stock of the Federal reserve bank issuing them.

Upon application of any Federal reserve bank, approved by the Federal Reserve Board, the Secretary of the Treasury may issue, in exchange for United States two per centum gold bonds bearing the circulation privilege, but against which no circulation is outstanding, one-year gold notes of the United States without the circulation privilege, to an amount not to exceed one half of the two per centum bonds so tendered for exchange, and thirty-year three per centum gold bonds without the circulation privilege for the remainder of the two per centum bonds so tendered: *Provided*, That at the time of such exchange the Federal reserve bank obtaining such one-year gold notes shall enter into an obligation with the Secretary of the Treasury binding itself to purchase from the United States for gold at the maturity of such one-year notes, an amount equal to those delivered in exchange for such bonds, if so requested by the Secretary, and at each maturity of one-year notes so purchased by such Federal reserve bank, to purchase from the United States such an amount of one-year notes as the Secretary may tender to such bank, not to exceed the amount issued to such bank in the first instance, in exchange for the two per centum United States gold bonds; said obligation to purchase at maturity such notes shall continue in force for a period not to exceed thirty years.

For the purpose of making the exchange herein provided for, the Secretary of the Treasury is authorized to issue at par Treasury notes in coupon or registered form as he may prescribe in denominations of one hundred dollars, or any multiple thereof, bearing interest at the rate of three per centum per annum, payable quarterly, such Treasury notes to be payable not more than one year from the date of their issue in gold coin of the present standard value, and to be exempt as to principal and interest from the payment of all taxes and duties of the United States except as provided by this Act, as well as from taxes in any form by or under State, municipal, or local authorities. And for the same purpose, the Secretary is authorized and empowered to issue United States gold bonds at par, bearing three per centum interest, payable thirty years from date of issue, such bonds to be of the same general tenor and effect and to be issued under the same general terms and conditions as the United States three per centum bonds without the circulation privilege now issued and outstanding.

Upon application of any Federal reserve bank, approved by the Federal Reserve Board, the Secretary may issue at par such three per centum bonds in exchange for the one-year gold notes herein provided for.

Bank Reserves

SEC. 19. Demand deposits within the meaning of this Act shall comprise all deposits payable within thirty days, and time deposits shall comprise all deposits payable after thirty days, and all savings accounts and certificates of deposit which are subject to not less than thirty days' notice before payment.

When the Secretary of the Treasury shall have officially announced, in such manner as he may elect, the establishment of a Federal reserve bank in any district, every subscribing member bank shall establish and maintain reserves as follows:

(a) A bank not in a reserve or central reserve city as now or hereafter defined shall hold and maintain reserves equal to twelve per centum of the aggregate amount of its demand deposits and five per centum of its time deposits, as follows:

In its vaults for a period of thirty-six months after said date five-twelfths thereof and permanently thereafter four-twelfths.

In the Federal reserve bank of its district, for a period of twelve months after said date, two-twelfths, and for each succeeding six months an additional one-twelfth, until five-twelfths have been so deposited, which shall be the amount permanently required.

For a period of thirty-six months after said date the balance of the reserves may be held in its own vaults, or in the Federal reserve bank, or in national banks in reserve or central reserve cities as now defined by law.

After said thirty-six months' period said reserves, other than those hereinbefore required to be held in the vaults of the member bank and in the Federal reserve bank, shall be held in the vaults of the member bank or in the Federal reserve bank, or in both, at the option of the member bank.

(b) A bank in a reserve city, as now or hereafter defined, shall hold and maintain reserves equal to fifteen per centum of the aggregate amount of its demand deposits and five per centum of its time deposits, as follows:

In its vaults for a period of thirty-six months after said date six-fifteenths thereof, and permanently thereafter five-fifteenths.

In the Federal reserve bank of its district for a period of twelve months after the date aforesaid at least three-fifteenths, and for each succeeding six months an additional one-fifteenth, until six-fifteenths have been so deposited, which shall be the amount permanently required.

For a period of thirty-six months after said date the balance of the reserves may be held in its own vaults, or in the Federal reserve bank, or in national banks in reserve or central reserve cities as now defined by law.

After said thirty-six months' period all of said reserves, except those hereinbefore required to be held permanently in the vaults of the member bank and in the Federal reserve bank, shall be held in its vaults or in the Federal reserve bank, or in both, at the option of the member bank.

(c) A bank in a central reserve city, as now or hereafter defined, shall hold and maintain a reserve equal to eighteen per centum of the aggregate amount of its demand deposits and five per centum of its time deposits, as follows:

In its vaults six-eighteenths thereof.

In the Federal reserve bank seven-eighteenths.

The balance of said reserves shall be held in its own vaults or in the Federal reserve bank, at its option.

Any Federal reserve bank may receive from the member banks as reserves, not exceeding one-half of each installment, eligible paper as described in section fourteen properly indorsed and acceptable to the said reserve bank.

If a State bank or trust company is required by the law of its State to keep its reserves either in its own vaults or with another State bank or trust company, such reserve deposits so kept in such State bank or trust company shall be construed, within the meaning of this section, as if they were reserve deposits in a national bank in a reserve or central reserve city for a period of three years after the Secretary of the Treasury shall have officially announced the establishment of a Federal reserve bank in the district in which such State bank or trust company is situate.

Except as thus provided, no member bank shall keep on deposit with any non-member bank a sum in excess of ten per centum of its own paid-up capital and surplus. No member bank shall act as the medium or agent of a non-member bank in applying for or receiving discounts from a Federal reserve bank under the provisions of this Act except by permission of the Federal Reserve Board.

The reserve carried by a member bank with a Federal reserve bank may, under the regulations and subject to such penalties as may be prescribed by the Federal Reserve Board, be checked against and withdrawn by such member bank for the purpose of meeting existing liabilities: *Provided, however,* That no bank shall at any time make new loans or shall pay any dividends unless and until the total reserve required by law is fully restored.

In estimating the reserves required by this Act, the net balance of amounts due to and from other banks shall be taken as the basis for ascertaining the deposits against which reserves shall be determined. Balances in reserve banks due to member banks shall, to the extent herein provided, be counted as reserves.

National banks located in Alaska or outside the continental United States may remain non-member banks, and shall in that event maintain reserves and comply with all the conditions now provided by law regulating them; or said banks, except in the Philippine Islands, may, with the consent of the Reserve Board, become member banks of any one of the reserve districts, and shall, in that event, take stock, maintain reserves, and be subject to all the other provisions of this Act.

SEC. 20. So much of sections two and three of the Act of June twentieth, eighteen hundred and seventy-four, entitled "An Act fixing the amount of United States notes, providing for a redistribution of the national-bank currency, and for other purposes," as provides that the fund deposited by any national banking association with the Treasurer of the United States for the redemption of its notes shall be counted as a part of its lawful reserve as provided in the Act aforesaid is hereby repealed. And from and after the passage of this Act such fund of five per centum shall in no case be counted by any national banking association as a part of its lawful reserve.

Bank Examinations

SEC. 21. Section fifty-two hundred and forty, United States Revised Statutes, is amended to read as follows:

The Comptroller of the Currency, with the approval of the Secretary of the Treasury, shall appoint examiners who shall examine every member bank at least twice in each calendar year and oftener if considered necessary: *Provided, however,* That the Federal Reserve Board may authorize examination by the State authorities to be accepted in the case of State banks and trust companies and may at any time direct the holding of a special examination of State banks or trust companies that are stockholders in any Federal reserve bank. The examiner making the examination of any national bank, or of any other member bank, shall have power to make a thorough examination of all the affairs of the bank, and in doing so he shall have power to administer oaths and to examine any of the officers and agents thereof under oath and shall make a full and detailed report of the condition of said bank to the Comptroller of the Currency.

The Federal Reserve Board, upon the recommendation of the Comptroller of the Currency, shall fix the salaries of all bank examiners and make report thereof to Congress. The expense of the examinations herein provided for shall be assessed by the Comptroller of the Currency upon the banks examined in proportion to assets or resources held by the banks upon the date of examination of the various banks.

In addition to the examinations made and conducted by the Comptroller of the Currency, every Federal reserve bank may, with the approval of the Federal reserve agent or the Federal Reserve Board, provide for special examination of member banks within its district. The expense of such examinations shall be borne by the bank examined. Such examinations shall be so conducted as to inform the Federal reserve bank of the condition of its member banks and of the lines of credit which are being extended by them. Every Federal reserve bank shall at all times furnish to the Federal Reserve Board such information as may be demanded concerning the condition of any member bank within the district of the said Federal reserve bank.

No bank shall be subject to any visitatorial powers other than such as are authorized by law, or vested in the courts of justice or such as shall be or shall have been exercised or directed by Congress, or by either House thereof or by any committee of Congress or of either House duly authorized.

The Federal Reserve Board shall, at least once each year, order an examination of each Federal reserve bank, and upon joint application of ten member banks the Federal Reserve Board shall order a special examination and report of the condition of any Federal reserve bank.

SEC. 22. No member bank or any officer, director, or employee thereof shall hereafter make any loan or grant any gratuity to any bank examiner. Any bank officer, director, or employee violating this provision shall be deemed guilty of a misdemeanor and shall be imprisoned not exceeding one year or fined not more than $5,000, or both; and may be fined a further sum equal to the money so loaned or gratuity given. Any examiner accepting a loan or gratuity from any bank examined by him or from an officer, director or employee thereof shall be deemed guilty of a misdemeanor and shall be imprisoned not exceeding one year or fined not more than $5,000, or both; and may be fined a further sum equal to the money so loaned or gratuity given; and shall forever threreafter be disqualified from holding office as a national-bank examiner. No national-bank examiner shall perform any other service for compensation while holding such office for any bank or officer, director, or employee thereof.

Other than the usual salary or director's fee paid to any officer, director, or employee of a member bank and other than a reasonable fee paid by said bank to such officer, director, or employee for services rendered to such bank, no officer, director, employee, or attorney of a member bank shall be a beneficiary of or receive, directly or indirectly, any fee, commission, gift, or other consideration for or in connection with any transaction or business of the bank. No examiner, public or private, shall disclose the names of borrowers or the collateral for loans of a member bank to other than the proper officers of such bank without first having obttained the express permission in writing from the Comptroller of the Currency or from the board of directors of such bank, except when ordered to do so by a court of competent jurisdiction, or by direction of the Congress of the United States, or of either House thereof, or of any committee of Congress or of either House duly authorized. Any person violating any provision of this section shall be punished by a fine of not exceeding $5,000 or by imprisonment not exceeding one year, or both.

Except as provided in existing laws, this provision shall not take effect until sixty days after the passage of this Act.

Sec. 23. The stockholders of every national banking association shall be held individually responsible for all contracts, debts and engagements of such association, each to the amount of his stock therein, at the par value thereof in addition to the amount invested in such stock. The stockholders in any national banking association who shall have transferred their shares or registered the transfer thereof within sixty days next before the date of the failure of such association to meet its obligations, or with knowledge of such impending failure, shall be liable to the same extent as if they had made no such transfer, to the extent that the subsequent transferee fails to meet such liability; but this provision shall not be construed to affect in any way any recourse which such shareholders might otherwise have against those in whose names such shares are registered at the time of such failure.

Loans on Farm Lands

Sec. 24. Any national banking association not situated in a central reserve city may make loans secured by improved and unencumbered farm land, situated within its Federal reserve district, but no such loan shall be made for a longer time than five years, nor for an amount exceeding fifty per centum of the actual value of the property offered as security. Any such bank may make such loans in an aggregate sum equal to twenty-five per centum of its capital and surplus or to one-third of its time deposits, and such banks may continue hereafter as heretofore to receive time deposits and to pay interest on the same.

The Federal Reserve Board shall have power from time to time to add to the list of cities in which national banks shall not be permitted to make loans secured upon real estate in the manner described in this section.

Foreign Branches

SEC. 25. Any national banking association possessing a capital and surplus of $1,000,000 or more may file application with the Federal Reserve Board, upon such conditions and under such regulations as may be prescribed by the said board, for the purpose of securing authority to establish branches in foreign countries or dependencies of the United States for the furtherance of the foreign commerce of the United States, and to act, if required to do so, as fiscal agents of the United States. Such application shall specify, in addition to the name and capital of the banking association filing it, the place or places where the banking operations proposed are to be carried on, and the amount of capital set aside for the conduct of its foreign business. The Federal Reserve Board shall have power to approve or to reject such application if, in its judgment, the amount of capital proposed to be set aside for the conduct of foreign business is inadequate, or if for other reasons the granting of such application is deemed inexpedient.

Every national banking association which shall receive authority to establish foreign branches shall be required at all times to furnish information concerning the condition of such branches to the Comptroller of the Currency upon demand, and the Federal Reserve Board may order special examinations of the said foreign branches at such time or times as it may deem best. Every such national banking association shall conduct the accounts of each foreign branch independently of the accounts of other foregn branches established by it and of its home office, and shall at the end of each fiscal period transfer to its general ledger the profit or loss accruing at each branch as a separate item.

SEC. 26. All provisions of law inconsistent with or superseded by any of the provisions of this Act are to that extent and to that extent only hereby repealed: *Provided,* Nothing in this Act contained shall be construed to repeal the parity provision or provisions contained in an Act approved March fourteenth, nineteen hundred, entitled "An Act to define and fix the standard of value, to maintain the parity of all forms of money issued or coined by the United States, to refund the public debt, and for other purposes," and the Secretary of the Treasury may for the purpose of maintaining such parity and to strengthen the gold reserve, borrow gold on the security of United States bonds authorized by section two of the Act last referred to or for one-year gold notes bearing interest at a rate of not to exceed three per centum per annum, or sell the same if necessary to obtain gold. When the funds of the Treasury on hand justify, he may purchase and retire such outstanding bonds and notes.

Sec. 27. The provisions of the Act of May thirtieth, nineteen hundred and eight, authorizing national currency associations, the issue of additional national-bank circulation, and creating a National Monetary Commission, which expires by limitation under the terms of such Act on the thirtieth day of June, nineteen hundred and fourteen, are hereby extended to June thirtieth, nineteen hundred and fifteen, and sections fifty-one hundred and fifty-three, fifty-one hundred and seventy-two, fifty-one hundred and ninety-one, and fifty-two hundred and fourteen of the Revised Statutes of the United States, which were amended by the Act of May thirtieth, nineteen hundred and eight, are hereby re-enacted to read as such sections read prior to May thirtieth, nineteen hundred and eight, subject to such amendments or modifications as are prescribed in this Act: *Provided, however,* That section nine of the Act first referred to in this section is hereby amended so as to change the tax rates fixed in said Act by making the portion applicable thereto read as follows:

National banking associations having circulating notes secured otherwise than by bonds of the United States, shall pay for the first three months a tax at the rate of three per centum per annum upon the average amount of such of their notes in circulation as are based upon the deposit of such securities, and afterwards an additional tax rate of one-half of one per centum per annum for each month until a tax of six per centum per annum is reached, and thereafter such tax of six per centum per annum upon the average amount of such notes.

SEC. 28. Section fifty-one hundred and forty-three of the Revised Statutes is hereby amended and re-enacted to read as follows: Any association formed under this title may, by the vote of shareholders owning two-thirds of its capital stock, reduce its capital to any sum not below the amount required by this title to authorize the formation of associations; but no such reduction shall be allowable which will reduce the capital of the association below the amount required for its outstanding circulation, nor shall any reduction be made until the amount of the proposed reduction has been reported to the Comptroller of the Currency and such reduction has been approved by the said Comptroller of the Currency and by the Federal Reserve Board, or by the organization committee pending the organization of the Federal Reserve Board.

SEC. 29. If any clause, sentence, paragraph, or part of this Act shall for any reason be adjudged by any court of competent jurisdiction to be invalid, such judgment shall not affect, impair, or invalidate the remainder of this Act, but shall be confined in its operation to the clause, sentence, paragraph, or part thereof directly involved in the controversy in which such judgment shall have been rendered.

SEC. 30. The right to amend, alter, or repeal this Act is hereby expressly reserved.

Title

The Federal Reserve Act.

1. Definition of "bank," "board," "district," etc.

Effective

As soon as practicable.

Federal Reserve Districts

Organization Committee composed of

1. Secretary of the Treasury.
2. Secretary of Agriculture.
3. Comptroller of the Currency.

Country to be divided into not less than 8 nor more than 12 districts.

1. Country to exclude Alaska.
2. Districts not necessarily coterminous with a state.

3. Districts may be readjusted by Federal Reserve Board.

4. Districts to be designated by number.

5. Each district to have a Federal Reserve City to be designated by the organization committee.

6. Organization committee may employ assistance.

Banks to become members.

1. All national banks required to become members.

2. Must signify their willingness to join within 60 days.

3. Within 30 days after receiving notice banks must subscribe 6 per centum of their capital and surplus to the capital of the reserve banks.

    (a) One-sixth to be payable on call.
    (b) One-sixth payable within three months.
    (c) One-sixth payable within six months.
    (d) Remainder subject to call.

4. Shareholders of Reserve Bank to be held responsible individually.

5. National banks failing to offer to come in the system within 60 days to cease to be a reserve agent.

    (a) Thirty days' notice to be given.

6. National banks failing to join within a year to be compelled to give up their national charters.

7. If banks fail to subscribe sufficient capital, stock of reserve bank may be offered to the public.

    (a) No one other than a bank may hold more than $25,000 stock in a reserve bank.

8. If not sufficient capital then raised, the United States government may subscribe.

Voting power of stock.

1. Stock held by others than banks not to have a voting power.

    (a) Reserve Board to regulate the transfers of this stock.

Size of banks.

1. No reserve bank to start with capital of less than $4,000,000.

2. Each reserve bank shall establish branches in its district.

    (a) Regulated by Board.
    (b) Reserve bank to designate manager of a branch.

Federal Reserve Banks

Application for a reserve bank to be filed with Comptroller of the Currency

1. By at least five banks in a district.

2. Organization certificate to be acknowledged before a judge, court of record, or notary public.

3. Certificates to state
   - (a) Name of reserve bank.
   - (b) Limits of the district.
   - (c) Location of reserve bank.
   - (d) Amount of capital stock.
   - (e) Etc.

Organization certificate gives power

1. To adopt a corporate seal.

2. To have twenty-year franchise.

3. To make contracts.

4. To have entity before law.

5. To appoint officers not enumerated by this act.

6. To prescribe by-laws.

7. To exercise specific and incidental powers.

8. To deposit government bonds and receive circulating notes from the Comptroller of the Currency.

9. Cannot exercise these powers until authorized by Comptroller of the Currency.

Board of directors of a Reserve Bank

1. To consist of three classes:

   Class A—Three members chosen by member banks.
   Class B—Three members representing commerce, agriculture and some other pursuit.
   Class C—Three members designated by Federal Reserve Board.

2. Directors of Class B and C not to be connected with any bank. B directors may, however, be shareholders.

3. No member of Congress may be member of Reserve Board, or director or officer of a reserve bank.

4. Class A and B directors elected by bank electors, each member bank having one vote.

5. Chairman of board of directors, (Federal Reserve Agent) one of Class C, to have tested banking experience.

6. One director of each class to retire each year—thereafter term of office is three years.

7. Method of selecting directors of Class A and B prescribed.
8. Specific qualifications required of Class C director.
9. Chairman to be "Federal reserve agent."
10. Chairman to have tested banking experience.
11. Deputy chairman—from Class C—to have tested banking experience.
12. Expenses to be paid by reserve banks.

Stock issues; increase of capital.

1. Shares, $100.
2. Stock increased as member banks increase or grow.
3. Shares held by member banks not to be transferred or hypothecated.
4. New shares and shares surrendered after organization to be paid at par plus dividend.
5. Failed and liquidated banks and capital decreases of member banks corresponds to increase and decrease in reserve bank capital.

Division of earnings.

1. Stockholders to receive 6 per cent. cumulative dividend.
   (a) First excepting expenses of reserve banks.

2. Remainder to go to Government.

   (a) One-half of earnings remaining after the payment of these obligations to create a surplus fund. Until surplus equals 40 per cent of capital of a reserve bank.

3. Secretary of Treasury may use net earnings to the government to add to gold reserve or to be used in liquidating the bonded debt.

4. Reserve banks exempt from taxation, except on real estate.

State banks

1. May become national banks.

   (a) By compliance with national banking law.
   (b) When not in contravention of state law.

2. State banks and trust companies may become members and retain state charters by applying to Federal Reserve Board for membership in the system.

   (a) Must conform to reserve and capital requirements of national banks.
   (b) Must conform to national law on limitation of liability.
   (c) Must make reports to Comptroller.
   (d) Federal Reserve Board may suspend, cancel or restore a state institution to membership.

Federal Reserve Board

To consist of seven members:

1. Secretary of the Treasury.
2. Comptroller of the Currency.
3. Five others appointed by President with consent of the Senate.
   (a) These to represent the country geographically, commercially and industrially.
   (b) The five to devote entire time to their duties and receive salary of $12,000 per annum.
   (c) Comptroller to receive $7,000, in addition to his present salary.

4. Secretary and Assistant Secretaries of the Treasury, Comptroller and members of Board not permitted to take office with a member bank during term of office or for two years after retiring.

5. At least two members must be experienced in banking.

6. One member to retire each second year, thereafter term is 10 years.

7. One of the five appointees to be designated by President as governor of the board.

Board to levy semi-annually upon reserve banks assessment to pay expenses and salaries of board.

Offices to be in Treasury Department, Washington, D. C.

No member of board may be connected with any bank.

President may fill vacancies during recess of Congress.

Powers of Secretary of Treasury not curtailed.

Federal Reserve Board to report to the Speaker of the House of Representatives annually.

Federal Reserve Board has the following powers:

1. To examine Federal Banks and publish weekly statement.
2. To permit or require one reserve bank to rediscount for another reserve bank.
3. To suspend for not over 30 days the reserve requirements.
   (a) A graduated tax to apply when reserves fall below 40 per cent.
4. To supervise the issue and retirement of reserve notes.

5. To add to number of reserve and central reserve cities.

6. To suspend or remove any officer or director of a reserve bank.

7. To require writing off of worthless assets of a reserve bank.

8. To suspend, for cause, and operate a reserve bank.

9. To require bonds of reserve agents.

10. To exercise general supervision over reserve banks.

11. To permit national banks to act as trustee, executor, administrator, or registrar of stocks and bonds.

12. To employ necessary assistants, etc.
    (a) Without civil service act.

Federal Advisory Council, an adjunct to the Board.

1. One member selected by each reserve bank.

2. Salary to be fixed by reserve bank.

3. Council to meet in Washington, D. C., at least four times a year.

4. Meetings oftener when called by the Board.

5. Council has the power:

   (a) To confer with Board on general business conditions.

   (b) To make representations concerning matters under the jurisdiction of the Board.

   (c) To make recommendations regarding discount rates, and other operations of reserve banks.

Operations of Federal Reserve Banks

Reserve banks are granted the power

1. To receive deposits from member banks.

2. To receive deposits from the United States.

3. To receive deposits from other reserve banks.

4. To discount notes of member banks growing out of commercial transactions.

5. To discount acceptances indorsed by a member bank.

   (a) Amount of acceptances not to exceed one-half of capital of member bank.

   (b) Amount of notes of one person not to exceed 10 per cent. of capital and surplus of member bank.

   (c) Amount of commercial notes not to exceed one-half paid-up capital and surplus of member bank.

6. Liability of member banks restricted.

7. Board may regulate discount operations of a reserve bank.

Open-market operations.

1. Reserve bank may purchase and sell in open market.

   (a) Cable transfers.

   (b) Bankers' acceptances.

   (c) Bills of exchange.

2. A reserve bank has power

   (a) To deal in gold coin and bullion.

   (b) Buy and sell bonds and notes of certain kinds.

   (c) Purchase and sell bills of exchange.

   (d) Establish rates of discount.

   (e) Establish exchange accounts at home and abroad.

Government deposits.

1. Secretary of Treasury may deposit public funds with reserve banks, and use reserve banks as fiscal agents.

   (a) Excepting five per cent. redemption fund.

   (b) National banks may still be government depositories.

Note issues.

1. Board to issue reserve notes to reserve banks.

    (a) Notes to be obligations of government.

    (b) Redeemable in gold at Treasury.

    (c) Redeemable in gold or lawful money at reserve bank.

2. Reserve banks to receive these notes upon filing notes and bills accepted for rediscount.

    (a) Board may call upon reserve bank for additional security.

3. Reserve bank to maintain reserve in gold or lawful money of 35 per cent of deposits.

    (a) Gold reserve against notes in circulation must be 40 per cent.

4. Reserve bank taxed 10 per cent on notes it issues of any other reserve bank.

5. Reserve bank to deposit with Treasury a redemption fund of at least 5 per cent.

6. Reserve bank may reduce outstanding liabilities by depositing with Treasury notes, gold, certificates, or lawful money.

7. Reserve agent to hold gold, certificates or lawful money for exchange for reserve notes.

8. Reserve bank may substitute collateral held by agent.

9. Comptroller to have dies prepared for engraving reserve notes.

    (a) Reserve banks to bear expense of engraving.

10. Reserve banks to clear checks

    (a) Received at par from members.

    (b) At par from other reserve banks.

    (c) Board to regulate charges exacted of member banks for clearing checks.

    (d) Board to regulate transfer of funds.

11. New national banks not to issue circulation based on bonds.

Government bonds to be refunded.

1. After two years from passage of this act and for twenty years thereafter a bank may retire its notes and sell its bonds held as security.

2. Applications for this to be filed with U. S. Treasurer.

3. Retiring bonds to be purchased by Federal Reserve Banks.

    (a) Bonds purchased in any one year not to exceed $25,000,000.

    (b) Reserve bank purchasing the bonds may issue circulating notes equal to par value of the bonds.

    (c) These circulating notes to be obligations of reserve banks.

4. Government may issue in exchange for outstanding 2 per cent bonds, against which no circulation is outstanding.

    (a) One-year 3 per cent treasury gold notes, 50 per cent interest.

    (b) Thirty-year 3 per cent bonds, 50 per cent.

Requirements of Banks

Country banks should hold reserves

1. Of 12 per cent on demand deposits.

2. Of 5 per cent on time deposits.

3. This reserve to be segregated as follows:

    (a) In vaults (Compulsory):

12 months	5-12
18 months	5-12
24 months	5-12
30 months	5-12
36 months	5-12
Thereafter	4-12

In Federal Reserve Bank (Compulsory):

12 months	2-12
18 months	3-12
24 months	4-12
30 months	5-12
36 months	5-12
Thereafter	5-12

(b) The remainder to be held for the first 36 months in either the vaults, reserve banks or in national banks in reserve cities or central reserve cities.

(c) Thereafter it may be held in vaults or in re-reserve banks.

Reserve city banks shall hold reserves

1. Of 15 per cent. on demand deposits.

2. Of 5 per cent on time deposits.

3. This reserve to be segregated as follows:

(a) In vaults (Compulsory):

12 months	6-15
18 months	6-15
24 months	6-15
30 months	6-15
36 months	6-15
Thereafter	5-15

In Federal Reserve Banks (Compulsory):

12 months	3-15
18 months	4-15
24 months	5-15
30 months	6-15
36 months	6-15
Thereafter	6-15

(b) The remainder to be held for the first 36 months in either vault, reserve banks or in banks in reserve or central reserve cities.

    (c)   Thereafter it may be held in vaults or in reserve banks.

Central reserve city banks shall hold reserves

1. Of 18 per cent on demand deposits.

2. Of 5 per cent on time deposits.

3. This reserve to be segregated as follows:

    (a)   In vaults (compulsory), 6-18 thereof.

    (b)   In reserve banks (compulsory), 7-18 thereof.

    (c)   Remainder in either own vaults or in reserve bank.

Reserves of state banks held in state banks to be considered as being held by reserve or central reserve city national banks.

1. A member bank could not rediscount with a Reserve association any paper endorsed by non-member bank except by permission of Federal Board.

Reserves in reserve banks may be checked against.

Banks in Alaska or outside the continental United States not required to come into the system.

Bank examinations.

1. Comptroller of the currency to authorize bank examinations.

2. Board to fix salaries of bank examiners.

3. A reserve bank may authorize the examination of a member bank within its district.

4. Board to order examination of Reserve Banks at least once a year.

No loan or gratuity may be extended an examiner by a bank.

No extra fee, etc., may be paid an officer or employee of a bank.

1. Effective 60 days after passage of this act.

Stockholders of banks are individually responsible.

Any country or reserve city bank may make farm loans.

1. Such loans may not be made by central reserve city banks.

2. Cannot be made for a time longer than 5 years.

3. Not to exceed 50 per cent of the value of the land.

4. Such loans not to exceed 25 per cent of a bank's capital and surplus or one-third of its time deposits.
5. Board may add to list of cities within which the banks may not loan on farm lands.

Foreign branches
1. May be established by a member bank with capital exceeding $1,000,000 upon application to the Board.
2. Branches under regulation of the Board.
3. Reports of branches to be filed with Comptroller.

Accounts of branches to be separate.

Nothing in this act to repeal the gold standard act.

Aldrich-Vreeland emergency currency act extended until June 30, 1915.
1. This act amended by reducing tax rate.

Miscellaneous

National banks permitted to reduce their capital.

If a court holds one section of this act unconstitutional, that shall not impair the remainder of the act.

Right to amend, alter or repeal is reserved.

INDEX

The Federal Reserve Act

The Federal Reserve Act

The Federal Reserve Act

The Federal Reserve Act

The Federal Reserve Act

Made in the USA
Las Vegas, NV
24 September 2023

78092557R00070